G000066208

INSIDE
WRIGHT

INSIDE WRIGHT

MY WORLD IN PICTURES

IAN WRIGHT

Hodder & Stoughton

The right of Ian Wright to be identified as the Author of
the Work has been asserted by him in accordance with the
Copyright, Designs and Patents Act 1988.
Copyright © 1994 Ian Wright.
First published in Great Britain in 1994 by Hodder & Stoughton
A division of Hodder Headline PLC

A Coronet paperback
10 9 8 7 6 5 4 3 2 1

All rights reserved. No part of this publication may be reproduced,
stored in a retrieval system, or transmitted in any form or by any means
without the prior written permission of the publisher, nor be otherwise
circulated in any form of binding or cover other than that in which it is
published and without similar condition being imposed on the
subsequent purchaser.
A C.I.P. catalogue record for this title is available from
the British Library.

0 340 587865

Graphic design by Design/Section
Printed and bound in Great Britain by
Butler & Tanner Ltd, Frome and London

Hodder and Stoughton Ltd
A Division of Hodder Headline PLC
338 Euston Road
London NW1 3BH

Contents

Introduction

Welcome to INSIDE WRIGHT. The game of football has so many different aspects to it that, while I can't pretend to cover them all, I hope this book will stir some memories, maybe get you thinking and perhaps raise a few smiles as I look over my life on and off the pitch.

The fact that I am a professional footballer is down to one decision I made as a twenty-one-year-old. After previous disappointments I was offered a trial with a then second-division club. For a brief moment I was afraid to take the gamble. I'd lost my job before when I'd taken time off to see if I could make the grade. But in the end I couldn't resist the challenge.

I'm glad the way things turned out, because football has been very good to me. I have seen many countries and met many people that I would probably otherwise have seen only on TV.

Being such a late starter gives me a huge appetite to make up for lost time. I've got fewer years than other players in which to cram my career. I desperately want to succeed. It's something that burns inside me - inside Wright.

Finally, I would like to thank David Bloomfield for helping me put this book together, and also my agents Jerome Anderson Management Ltd, for their support.

Ian Wright
Arsenal FC and England

CHAPTER ONE

SCHOOLBOY HEROES

All kids have heroes - people they admire and respect. I was no different. There was a handful of players I tried to copy in the playground. When I got to play professional football myself I would still think about the reasons why I had liked those players. I can still remember all the magic moments of skill they had showed.

When you were a youngster and you'd just scored a goal - perhaps it had involved a great mazy dribble around all their defenders - you would put your hands up, waving to an imaginary crowd, and for a brief moment pretend you were Stan Bowles or Laurie Cunningham.

Stan the Man was a great player and a great entertainer. He had a lovely left foot, great ball control. A flair player. He always looked as if he was doing just whatever he liked on the pitch. He was concerned that he looked good and you could see that he really loved using his skills to show up the defenders who tried to kick him.

When the ball came to Stan he controlled it dead. Straight away, no mistake. He always had his shirt out and with his long hair he looked a rogue and a rebel. But he could really play, he would make terrific passes for his team-mates, so he wasn't selfish and he also scored a lot of goals, especially for QPR. Great goals. Somehow a Stan Bowles' goal was a special one: it just looked different from everybody else's.

Big Cyrille Regis and Laurie Cunningham were two other players I really looked up to. You just had to admire them. In the 1970s it wasn't easy for black players. The situation is much, much better now. But you have to say that there was racism in those days and these players, they coped with all the pressures. And that was a great help to me because I would look at their example and say to myself that I could make it as a player as well.

Nowadays it's just normal for teams to have black players. Although Cyrille was a big, strong centre-forward and scored a lot of goals using brute strength he had a very calm temperament. Nothing seemed to annoy him, he just got on with the game. Defenders could say things or try and foul him but he would take no notice and nearly always scored a goal. The best way to shut people up.

I don't think I'm like that. I really wish I could be more like Cyrille. I would certainly get fewer bookings, though I know I don't get anywhere near the number some people think.

Laurie Cunningham, who died in a tragic car accident in Spain a few years ago, was also an inspiration. Great, silky skills, he loved to use his speed and trickery. He played for Orient and West Bromwich Albion and was also a big success when he played for Real Madrid.

The one, the only, Stanley Bowles. Stan the Man had magic in those boots, he had ball control like no one else. He was a major star in the 1970s, a real hero to me. He loved to have a bet and it was said if he could pass a betting shop like he could pass a ball he would be a very rich man.

Goalscorers know we have to take the knocks if we are to get the goals but this Chilean defender seems determined to dish it out. Gerd Muller was one of the best goalscorers the world has ever seen. He was top scorer, with ten goals for West Germany, in the 1970 World Cup and scored literally hundreds of goals for Bayern Munich.

Mild-mannered Cyrille Regis - so like me in so many ways! No, but it's true I did try to model myself on him, I always admired his temperament, but he was the original. Most people think I've got a little way to go yet.

The late Laurie Cunningham had every skill and talent in the book and a few extra he invented just for himself. He was the smoothest runner you ever did see.

I think that as I've developed as a player I've tried to take a little of each of these players' attributes. I liked Stan and Laurie for their flair, Gerd for his out-and-out goalscoring and Cyrille because he was a great pioneer for black players in England and had strength, power and skill combined.

Laurie and Cyrille played together at West Brom when Ron Atkinson was manager. In 1979 they finished third in the League behind Liverpool and Nottingham Forest and were on TV many times. I always tried to watch them because there was something to learn each and every time you saw them play.

A very different type of player that I liked was Gerd Muller. He was the great striker for Bayern Munich and West Germany in the 1970s. It was very difficult to see what he was doing in a match: he never really seemed to do anything but somehow you knew he would score a goal. Maybe you wouldn't see him for ages but he could suddenly appear and be there to knock the ball in.

I don't think he ever scored a great individual goal but, as everyone knows, they all count. He had really quick instincts and would get his head or foot there before the defenders could. I liked him because he was so single-minded. He knew what his job was and he was the best at doing it.

In every playground game of football there would be someone who was a goal-hanger. He would just stand near the goal and do nothing but try and score a goal. We would always calls this person 'Gerd Muller'.

It would be really great to think that occasionally a goal is scored in the playground and the kid thinks he did that just like Ian Wright.

I also had and still have a great respect for Pele. He was really my Mum's favourite but I've seen all the videos of the fantastic Brazilian team of 1970 and I think she is a good judge. He was the greatest. But I am just a little too young to remember him in his prime so for me it was Stan, Cyrille, Laurie and Gerd who were my heroes and whom I pretended to be.

CHAPTER TWO

STRIKING OUT

The first position I made my own was as a left-winger. I was so skinny I couldn't play as a central striker and always seemed to get knocked off the ball. I'm stronger now and can take whatever centre-backs want to dish out.

Out on the wing I would always be shouting for the ball. I would face the defenders and take them on, trying to use my pace to my advantage.

The star on my Sunday side, St Paul's, was Danny Wallace. He was the player that other teams would try to stop. He was in the limelight - not me, stuck out on the left wing. We played together between the ages of eleven and fifteen. Then on the TV just a year later he was in the Southampton first team scoring a goal against Liverpool.

There were loads of scouts at our games. I knew they had come to see Danny but I would try and put on a show so that perhaps I would get a trial at a professional club. The manager of our team, Ernie Hutchins, I'm sure used to try and turn these scouts away because he wanted his best players to stay and win trophies and not keep going off for trials with other clubs. Ernie's tactics paid off: we used to win Cup Finals by scores like 6-0 and 13-1.

Still, it's good going for two players from that

Brighton and Hove Albion turned me down when I was a nineteen-year-old. At the time I was on the floor but when I saw the kit I would have had to wear all of a sudden life didn't seem so bad. Can you honestly imagine me wearing that? Steve Foster is the unfortunate model for what must be the worst kit ever.

Danny was a teenage sensation in Sunday morning soccer. All the scouts would come to see him play. Poor skinny Ian Wright had to play on the left wing because he wasn't strong enough to play in the centre.

I hope this is how Palace fans remember me. I scored a lot of goals for them and I'm grateful for the opportunity but for some reason they don't seem to like me now.

one Sunday team to have played for Manchester United and Arsenal and both to have played for England.

At my school, Samuel Pepys in south-east London, a teacher called Mr McCarthy gave me a lot of encouragement. He was great. He would often have a bit of advice to pass on and I remember many of the things he said even now. The main thing that still sticks in my mind is that you don't have to blast the ball as hard as you can to score. If you break the back of the net it's not as if it counts double. You can pass the ball into the net. I thought about what he said and it sounded just right. It helps you to keep cool and in control when you get a chance to score.

By the time I was nineteen I was beginning to think that a career as a professional footballer was passing me by. I had seen Danny make the grade and many youngsters were taken on by a club at sixteen.

Then out of the blue I got a trial at Brighton. I played in two reserve games, scored in both and played well, but still I wasn't offered a contract.

I thought my last chance had come and gone. I found out later that the club had financial problems, but they could have signed me for nothing - then.

It was another two years before my next chance came, this time with Crystal Palace. A successful trial soon led to first team duty.

I was glad to leave my job on the building site behind, and playing football for £100 a week seemed heaven. But I certainly had not 'made it': I had just got my foot on the ladder and very quickly I could tell that I was on the bottom rung and had a long way to go.

Most players are with clubs from schooldays: I missed perhaps five years, but if I look on the bright side it could be that this has helped me never to lose my enthusiasm for the game.

I call it the Peter Beardsley theory. He says that when the season has finished he would like just two weeks off before starting to train and play again. I think if you enjoy something you just want to keep doing it.

CHAPTER THREE

FIRST SIGNING

I'd never really been one for collecting footballers' autographs, but at a prize-giving ceremony when my Sunday team, St Paul's, had won everything in sight, Mark Aizlewood of Charlton Athletic and Wales was kind enough to present the trophies.

Seeing that there was a professional footballer standing in front of me and because all my team-mates were getting his autograph I thought I might as well get it too. He seemed a really nice guy and took time to talk to all of us.

What was so funny was that just a year and a bit later I was playing against him for Crystal Palace.

Now Mark is a very big central defender and likes to make it known to strikers that he is around.

So in a very short time I had gone from shaking his hand to being on the end of a lot of crunching challenges. Still, revenge is always sweet, and I do remember that I scored a goal in that game.

Mark Aizlewood's autograph is the only one in my collection, but very soon after I got it I gave him a reason to remember my name.

Now it's my turn to sign autographs. 'Ian Wright' is not too bad to sign - only nine letters - but I like the way Brazilian players' nick-names seem to be used as their real names, like Rai, Zico and Pele. It must take them half the time to sign their names. Any suggestions for a three-letter nickname?

CHAPTER FOUR

CAREER OPPORTUNITIES

I used to box for a club called St Thomas Apostle in Peckham. I wasn't the greatest so I tell anyone who asks that the reason I stopped was that I didn't want my fine features messed about.

But I do like to go and see a top fight. Nigel Benn is a relation of Paul Ince so he's always the guy I like to see finish on top.

I was a reasonable basketball player, nothing fantastic. I was a 'second six', which is not in the first five, but I was ready to come on at any time - a substitute really. I could move quickly enough: I'd move the ball, a bit like a midfield player, up towards those who could really do something. But to play at the top level you have to be a lot taller than I am.

I have watched quite a few of Nigel Benn's fights. As he is Paul Ince's cousin I'm under strict orders to shout him home. He is a winner and I can identify with that.

My boxing stance is a very defensive one! I've no objection to putting my head in when defenders' boots are flying but to volunteer to be punched seems a strange career to me.

I'm trying to find a basket to prac-tise my slam-dunking! Actually I've just scored a hat-trick against Southampton and I'm showing Ken Monkou, their centre-back, where the ball has gone.

Michael Jordan is quite a bit taller than me. I stand 5ft 9in so he towers above me. Obviously, height can be an advantage in football but every forward line will find room for you, whatever your height, if you are quick and nimble enough. Look at Romario and Bebeto of Brazil: hardly giants, are they?

CHAPTER FIVE

PLAYING FOR THE ARSENAL

One of the best ways to judge the standard of a club is to listen to what former players say about it. Anybody who has played for the Arsenal always speaks highly of 'the Gunners'. If a player has been sold by the club, or if he had only a limited run with the first team, he may think the manager or coaching staff didn't give him a fair deal, but you'll never hear him blasting off at the club itself.

The reason is that with the Arsenal you are treated like an adult. You can't say this of all the clubs - some have silly rules. But I've found George Graham very fair in all my dealings with him. The only condition he makes is that you do your job to the best of your ability - and I have no argument with that approach. I love his sense of fairness. It was a big factor in my decision to sign for the Arsenal until I'm thirty-six. The club has given me everything and I intend to repay George and repay the club.

When I signed I soon wished I could have joined earlier. That's how impressed I was from the very first. My journey from being a Sunday morning footballer to the marble halls of Highbury had been a long and painful one, working on a building site and having trials with other clubs. My story was almost the complete opposite of Tony Adams' path to fame. He's been with Arsenal so long you could be forgiven for thinking he was born here. He worked his way to the very top at the club and he must be just about the most successful club captain ever.

When Tony is on the pitch he is totally committed to the job in hand. Winning matches and trophies for the Arsenal is what makes him tick. He is the leader, and he inspires us with his attitude. Captain Fantastic! Look at him playing for England now - he's just getting better and better. The US World Cup would have seen him establish himself on the biggest stage of all. I think everyone at Highbury is genuinely proud of him when he puts on an England shirt, and he does us credit too.

People often tell me I'm trying to break the mould of what an Arsenal player should be. I don't agree. I have the greatest respect for this club and I feel very much a part of everything that goes on at Highbury.

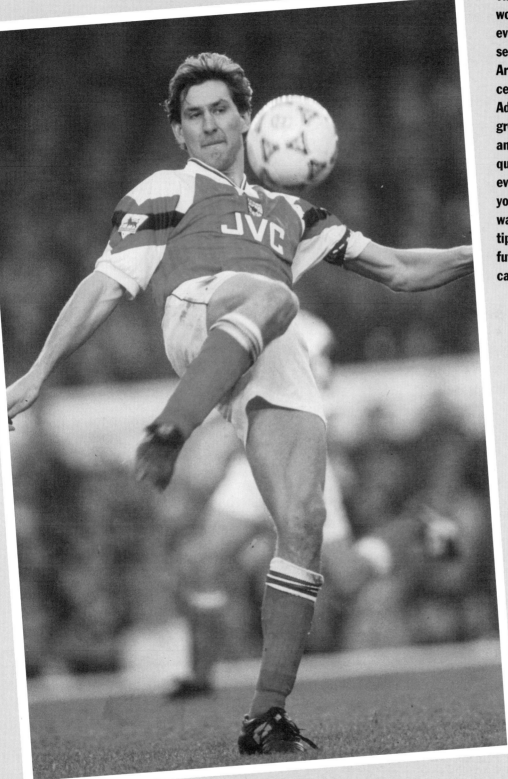

This man would give everything to see the Arsenal successful. Tony Adams is a great leader and I can quite see why even as a youngster he was being tipped as a future England captain.

John Jensen, a tireless worker in our midfield, but not yet a great goalscorer for Arsenal! He hit a great goal for Denmark against Germany in Euro '92 and once he gets one for us more will undoubtedly follow.

I'm proud to be a Gunner. I can't believe they used to play in boots like these. Those we play in today weigh just a few ounces. If FIFA really want to increase the number of goals they should insist defenders play in them.

When I finally retire, I know that I will be made welcome whenever I want to watch a game here. I don't get that impression of my previous club, Crystal Palace. It's not that the club itself seems unwelcoming, but I don't feel the fans would want me back. It's a shame, because the club is still my 'local'. I don't think I can explain this attitude. It could be jealousy or resentment. I wasn't exactly shouting from the rooftops about wanting to leave them: in fact I went on signing contracts with Crystal Palace when I knew other clubs were interested in getting me to play for them.

Palace got over £2 million for me when I was transferred, so if you add on the goals I got for them as well, I think I left them well in profit.

I was pleased that Steve Bould played for England last season. I don't like the idea that it was just a reward for long service, either. He deserved to play, and did very well too from what I saw.

Everybody is waiting for John Jensen to score his first goal for Arsenal. I would like him to score five on the spin and then all his critics would soon forget his dry spell. But when he does get his first goal our commercial department will make a fortune in celebration T-shirts. I'm glad it doesn't bother John. I would see it worrying a lesser man, but he's so confident and in training he scores some great goals. It's just that, in matches, a lot of his good shots seem to get deflected. His luck must change, I'm sure.

Perhaps Steve Bould, Nigel Winterburn and Alan Smith do not get quite the publicity their displays warrant. But make no mistake: their contribution is totally recognised by the players and managers at Highbury - and, I hope, by all Arsenal fans.

Playing for the Arsenal is special. You have certain standards to live up to. We are constantly reminded who we are, and who we represent. 'Remember who you are!' we are told, and it's a good motto. I am very conscious of this, and I'm certainly not proud of any 'disagreements' I might have had with referees. It's an area of my game that is definitely improving, and at least I don't get into off-the-field scrapes. I do try to remember who I represent.

CHAPTER SIX

HIDDEN TALENTS

I like to think I have a few hidden talents. Right now I'm taking saxophone lessons. My teacher, Vic Davis, has got me playing jazz and blues. Because I'm enjoying the lessons and the practice it's a pleasure to learn and I don't ever get bored with it, which with me is saying something.

Apart from my teacher no one will hear me play until I'm up to a really good standard. One day, when I've mastered the instrument, I'll play before a few people. I can't wait to see their faces. 'Wow,' they'll say, 'I didn't know you could play!'

Of course when I was at school I didn't take any notice of music lessons, but now I'm so very keen to make up for lost time. I am determined to learn to play the piano very soon as well. When I get a bigger house and bigger front room, I'll have the right place to put my piano.

I've got a young son, Stacey. I'm going to insist that he takes piano lessons though he doesn't know it yet as he's not even a year old. I hope he thanks me when he's older.

I also like to sing. Being the modest chap I am, I leave it to others to say if I'm any good or not, but I remember when the entire England squad each had a go on a karaoke machine and I brought the house down with the soul number 'Just My Imagination'. I suppose it's the performer or entertainer in me coming out. I did enjoy the applause.

There aren't too many famous singers and saxophonists: not even I can do both at the same time!

Chris Lowe, of the Pet Shop Boys, and I got together to make a record in 1993. He's a big Arsenal fan but had no idea that I could sing well enough to carry the record. When I went to the studio at his house all the engineers were totally amazed. I get a thrill out of people's expectations of me being totally wrong.

Chris's playing on the keyboards is absolutely brilliant. It's limitless what he can do, and when you add in the computers - well! It's really something else.

When the record, 'Do The Right Thing', was released it was kept under wraps who was singing, so that made it even better when people said they liked it. It wasn't a Number One smash hit, but it was very satisfying to see it in the Top Thirty.

The lyrics were very important to me. Basically they talk about not giving up, despite the pressures you feel you are under. Anyone can just give in and give up, but that isn't my style. Around that time I felt that some of the press were hounding me and it was good for me to have some outlet.

One of the biggest let-downs about England not making the USA for the World Cup was that the squad didn't have a chance to make a record. I think in 1990 with 'World in Motion' England set the standards for other football records to be judged against. I want to sing for England!

I definitely want to make more records, but it has to be the right project, so I'm a bit like an actor waiting for a good part to come along.

I think being a footballer or a pop star are so alike in many ways. As a kid you want to be one or the other. I know I did.

Entertaining the public is what both jobs are about. Football's top priority is to win but you want to go about it in the right way; and the target as a pop star must be to reach number one, but at the same time achieve success in your own way.

Many musicians like football and I know it's true the other way round too, so maybe I'll be lucky and some good music offers will come my way.

Another ambition I have is to be an actor. I would like to do comedy acting. The thought of making people laugh really appeals to me. I think that it would be unique because I just can't think of any actor who was once a professional footballer. And by acting I do not mean falling down in the box to get a penalty!

My style of acting would be something like Eddie Murphy's. He always seems to get the girl and always has just the right thing to say.

It's great fun having a few outside interests, but I wouldn't let them get in the way of my football. It's what I enjoy most. I love training, I love playing and I would never do anything that harmed my career. It's just too important to me.

There's something about the saxophone that looks the business, even if you can't play a note. However, I'm not making any public appearances until I've mastered at least two!

Chris Lowe, of the Pet Shop Boys, was a big help in the studio but I was more nervous than if I'd been playing at Wembley. At the end of the session I was more exhausted than after a Cup Final.

CHAPTER SEVEN

Tips For Young Strikers

Maybe it's the most obvious thing to say, but in football you should try not to lose the ball easily. At the top level it can be a very long time before you get a chance to regain possession, so don't give it away cheaply. For example, the goalkeeper may come out and collect a cross but at least you have made an attempt on goal. But a poorly placed pass can put you in all sorts of trouble.

To keep possession of the ball you need to have good control yourself, but it's just as important that you have team-mates who make themselves available for you to pass to them.

As a striker you need to concentrate on hitting the target. Again this is just simple advice but if you hurry your shot and the ball flies over the bar you're not doing your team much good. Try to minimise the number of times you miss the target.

In a group of players, any group, there will always be a few flair players. They just seem to have more natural ability than their team-mates. But having more skill does not in itself make them better players. To be a good flair player you have to put in your fair share of hard work.

You should never come off the pitch asking yourself if you could have done any more for your team.

You need to establish a base, a platform to show off your talents, and you only do that by

The Joy of Teamwork. All those hours of training, working on moves and being barked at by coaches pay off when a goal is scored.

hard graft. Don't just be a flair player; be a good flair player.

Goalscorers need to be brave. It is essential. Sometimes by accident, sometimes not, you will get hurt, but the joy of scoring an important goal will make that kick in the face just a minor problem.

In matches I am always looking and waiting for an opportunity to go one-on-one with the goalkeeper. In training this is the exact moment I prepare myself for. You need bottle in these situations. I wait until the very last moment. I have in my mind to put the chance to the goalkeeper's left, because if he is right handed it will take him longer to get down on that side.

If the goalkeeper dives one way before I'm ready to shoot, it just makes my job easier because I then put the ball in the other corner. I can tell you that the thrill I get scoring goals is the same now as when I was thirteen.

It is a great advantage as a striker to have a partner you are happy to play with. All strikers are a little selfish - I think that's why we are goalscorers - but if another player is in a much better position than you to score, you MUST pass to him.

People who understand the game can tell a mile off those players who shoot all the time and never pass. It always backfires because their team-mates will just begin not to pass to them. Don't be like that as a player. It makes you a much better player if you create chances for others and, almost by magic, you will find that chances will be made for you.

Take it softly sometimes. Accuracy is your number-one goal. You've more chance of hitting the target by side-footing the ball.

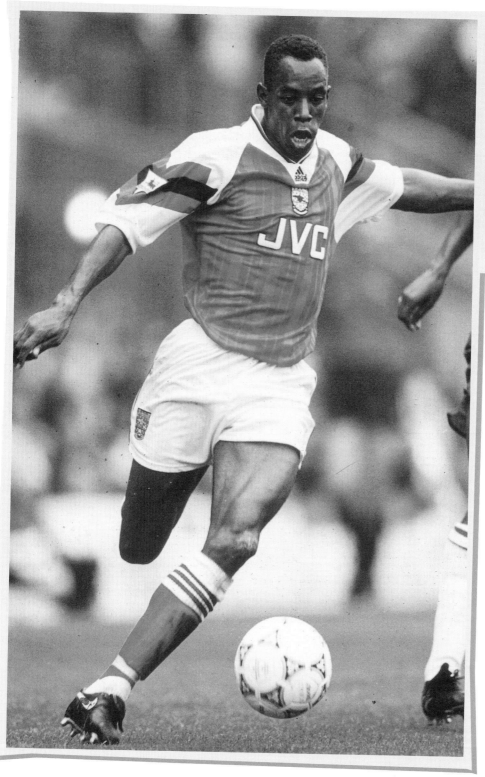

For ninety minutes I am totally focused on the job in hand. I've got just two things in mind:-
i) Am I in a good enough position to shoot?
ii) Is there anyone in a better position than me?
If there is I must pass to him.

Ian Wright - Arsenal FC and England.

Behind you! Behind you!

'There is no such thing as an easy game in international football.'

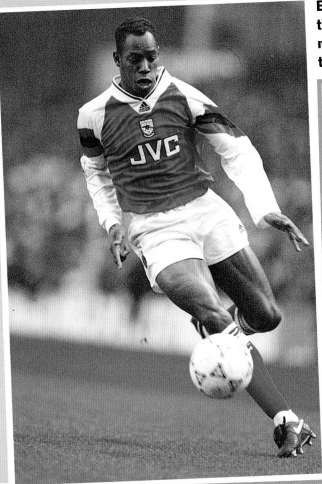

Eyes on the ball, mind on the job.

The honour of playing for England fills me with pride.

Cool Notes.

The World Cup has seen some strange hair-styles but this one is out of this world.

I had some good times on the building site, but football's altogether more fun!

Brazil, World Cup Winners 1994, World Champions for a record fourth time.

Romario, my
Player of the
World Cup
1994, going
for goal as
usual.

Stefan Schwarz (right) of Sweden and now Arsenal must be a quality player to come out on top in a challenge with the great Gheorghe Hagi.

Roberto Baggio's goals got Italy to the Final. Forget the penalty miss - without him Italy would never have got that far.

Maradona takes to the air before a routine drug test brought him and Argentina down to the ground with a bump.

CHAPTER EIGHT

DRESSED UP TO THE NINES

I don't think it's vanity or anything like that, but I do feel it's important to spend time on looking smart, especially if you are going to a function representing your club or your country. I suppose really you are showing good manners to your host in taking the trouble, rather than just turning up in a pair of jeans.

I do believe that if you look good you will feel good, too. Also, as a professional footballer, virtually everywhere you go you are on show, and I don't like it when I hear bad things about smartness because I think, by and large, footballers are well turned out.

Public figures are being judged all the time. People will pay you a compliment if you look good, but they also feel entitled to say you look a right mess if that's their opinion. Fair enough, I suppose.

When I was young, I couldn't afford to buy as many shoes and clothes as I do now, but I would always try to buy good quality even if it meant buying far fewer things. It just seemed to make sense to me.

I love a good shoe. I won't tell you how many pairs I've got at home, as it might sound greedy. But I promise you it's quite a few. Church and Grenson are my favourite two makes. On first impression you could say they were expensive, but these shoes will definitely last longer and still look good years after you've bought them. They age very well.

I've got a good eye for shoes. Even at a distance I can often recognise the brand someone is wearing. I can't help it but, after I've been introduced to someone, I quickly try to sneak a look at his shoes. You can tell a lot by a man's shoes, I think!

It doesn't compare to scoring a goal, but wearing a new pair of shoes for the first time is a big thrill. The first time you put that leather on the pavement is a great feeling.

I also wear my football boots around the house. No, I do not think I'm mad! I want to feel very comfortable with them and walking on the carpet seems to do the trick. They are, after all, the tools of my trade. Also I like to look at them in the mirror to see that they are just right. Deborah, my wife, keeps telling me to take them off because of what they are doing to the carpet.

The look of the 1930s gangster is a style that appeals to me. A good old black-and-white gangster movie is hard to beat. By the way, my Jimmy Cagney impression is rubbish.

I like to wear suits, sometimes with a waistcoat. I don't think you need to be tied to one particular style: the American college-boy look and the traditional English suit are two of my favourites. I also consider a good pair of cuff-links - nothing too fancy, mind - can make all the difference.

I am very lucky that I can afford to have a tailor make some of my suits. He used to be a West End tailor but has since moved to Luton. Sousters of Luton will do for me. They have made suits in a very English style for generations, so I know I'm buying quality.

It might take ages to think of a design, followed by great, lengthy discussions about how to turn that idea into a suit, and then get it made, but the finished creation is worthwhile. They know I like the trousers to hang just right so you can see the shoes.

One of my big favourites is a 1930s gangster-style suit. There are enough pin-stripes on it for people to think at first glance that I may be an accountant. But if they look closer they see there's something just a little extra about it.

Sousters also made me a very loud tartan waistcoat with crested buttons. I'm very careful not to wear it north of the border, in case I was thought to be a secret Scotland supporter.

I'm so pleased that I can afford to do these things. I have plenty of enthusiasm and a lot of drive, but I can't think of any other career that would have given me as much as football has given me.

Terry Venables had just called me into the England squad so I had to dress for the occasion. Casual but smart and one of my many baseball caps to top it off.

I'd trained to be a plasterer but I was a bit of a cowboy. Apparently some of my handiwork stands to this day...

CHAPTER NINE

DEFENDERS I RESPECT

There isn't a defender that I dislike playing against. In fact the bigger the name, the more I relish the challenge. I enjoy testing myself against the best, and in England that means Des Walker and Gary Pallister.

Every centre back in the premier league has his qualities. But I remember my meetings with Des and Gary the most. I hope the defenders don't look forward to marking me. If they do they should know that they will have a hard but fair contest. I have got no time for forwards who use their elbows to try to get an advantage. It's not something in my game and I wish it were not in the game at all.

If I'm playing against Des we will probably phone each other a couple of days before the match. We are both getting mentally ready for our personal contest. Sometimes when I've played against Des I haven't had a kick all game. Even when I got the ball from a throw-in Des would suddenly appear and take it away from me. This happened in one game at Highbury but I managed to score in something like the ninety-fifth minute. At the end of the game Des came over to me and said, 'OK, you won that one'.

Defenders have to watch strikers for the whole game. One slight slip and we can score. I give everything I can during a match: I never go easy and think, 'Oh well, I'll score next week'. It's just not my approach to try and keep something back for the next match. That would be a really bad habit to get into!

When we play Manchester United, Gary is usually given the job of marking me. Of course he's great in the air, physically very strong and those very long legs of his often make dramatic last-ditch tackles possible. Against Gary I look to get a ball over the top and, while I'm quicker over ten to fifteen yards, over twenty yards Gary can usually beat me. His strength begins to tell.

Every goal is something you have to work very hard for, but if you manage to score against either of these two men, you know you're still managing to meet the challenge.

Another great favourite of mine is Gary Mabbutt. You must be joking if you think he's a soft touch just because he's getting a little older. He has been a giant in the centre of Spurs' defence for many years and I was pleased when he managed to secure a new two-year contract this summer. There is no doubt in my mind that Spurs would have missed him.

Gary is one hundred per cent fair in all the challenges he makes. He goes for the ball fairly at all times. Not like some defenders I could mention

- but I would rather not give them publicity. They know who they are.

I am very much looking forward to the introduction here of the new World Cup ruling on tackles from behind. It will help forwards, there is no doubt about that. And I mean to make defenders pay!

So many times, when you are playing in those first five minutes, you know you are going to be tackled very heavily from behind - and I'm putting it as politely as I can. The top strikers have always taken those knocks, got up and carried on. But it will be a big relief to know that this sort of tackle will be punished by a booking or even a red card in future.

Always, always defenders! This would be an easy game without them. A hop and a skip and I'm past these tough-tackling Turks.

Des is heading our way. Here he has his eyes locked on the ball. When we play each other he keeps me firmly in his sights. But if he so much as blinks when a cross comes in I'll make him pay.

An unusual picture of Gary. This one manages to get his long legs all in. You look next time you see his picture in the paper: they just don't seem to have the room.

CHAPTER TEN

PLAYING FOR ENGLAND

When I hear that I have been picked for an England squad I get the same buzz I did the very first time. It's excellent.

First of all I look forward to being with the lads. I share a room with Incey, and we really do have a lot of laughs. We have loads to talk about. We always rabbit on about what medals we have won lately. Incey calls Manchester United 'Medal United'. I try to argue with him but it's hard because Medal United has been very successful. But Arsenal have won a lot of medals as well. It's those two championship medals of his that I would really like to get my hands on.

Everybody at an England get-together calls Paul and me 'The Twins'. David Platt started it and the nickname has stuck. It all began in America when England went on tour there in 1993. The idea was that it would prepare us for the World Cup a year later. Great idea: if only we'd qualified.

Anyway Paul and I went shopping in this massive mall in Detroit. Wherever we went we liked the same clothes so we ended up buying the same things. We wore the gear that night and we looked so smart. David just shouted 'Oh no! here come The Twins'.

In training we always try to do something different from all the others. The lads expect this and we try hard not to let them down.

I remember one time when we cut down our tracksuit bottoms into long shorts. It was nice and cool on our legs. Other times we will wear goalkeepers' socks instead of the usual ones.

Some people just like to be different, I guess. It doesn't do any harm and if a few people get to smile a bit more then - great!

(I hope the England kit-man is not reading this because now he'll know who cuts the legs off his tracksuits and why he can never find enough goalkeepers' socks!)

I've no doubt in my mind that my first goal for England was the highlight of my career. It was a World Cup qualifier in Poland in 1993 and I'd come on as a late sub and scored to make it 1-1. I've got a lot of years left in these legs and I know I'm going to score many more goals, but right now I have to say that was the highlight.

It was a really great feeling. I really thought we would build on that and make it to the US.

Ince and Wright show off their latest designer fashions - cut off tracksuit bottoms. If the England kit-man sees this we'll be in trouble because he's always asking questions about who took a pair of scissors to his kit.

Until then I had been getting so much stick from so many people. I knew that I'd played well for England, set up goals for others, run my heart out, but just hadn't managed to score. (It doesn't need me to remind anybody what happened in our next game in Norway.)

There is a lot of talk in the game about England playing Scotland again. It's a good idea. I would like to see it and I'm sure many, many other fans would as well. England and Scotland have played each other over more than a hundred years, and I know all the players would like to be part of this bit of football history. It would be a game of passion, a chance to be really patriotic. Yes, that definitely appeals to me.

I am quite pleased with myself. Behind me is David Bloomfield from the FA. Looking the English gent he is, he's about to point me in the direction of a TV crew for an interview.

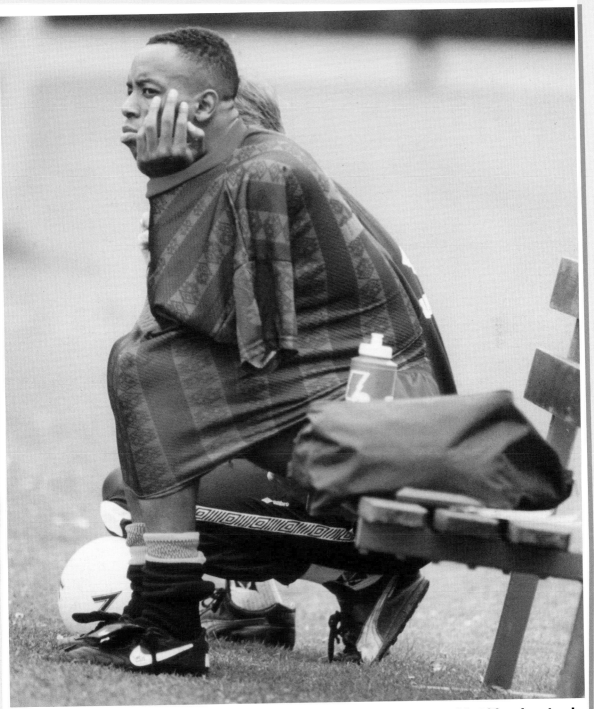

I'll sit on the bench if asked but it's only natural to want to be in the starting line-up. I look a bit glum here, not my usual expression when I'm with England.

The top of your chosen profession, that's how you feel when you represent England. It's always a great honour.

An excellent way to warm up before the serious training begins is to engage in a spot of mud-wrestling. Gazza from Dunstan is my opponent.

My first for England, the ball is on its way into the net and I touched it last! This goal put us level in Katowice against Poland and our World Cup hopes were still alive.

Terry is talking so I'm listening. They say that the best coaches have eyes in the back of their heads so I'd better watch my step. He's probably noticed already that I'm wearing goalkeepers' socks.

CHAPTER ELEVEN

STRIKERS I ADMIRE

Striker is a specialist position, and the success or failure of a team will depend to a large extent on its strikers. They are a sort of club within a club, and there is a lot of personal contact and respect among the members of our profession. Andy Cole for one is often on the phone to me, and I do get a thrill when he scores (provided it's not against Arsenal), especially if the goal is a result of some move we might have discussed.

I am not a teenager just coming into the game: I like to think I'm an established figure now, and that's the reason so many young players ask my advice. It's a nice compliment, and just as Chris Waddle and Mark Bright helped me with my game, I enjoy passing on any useful tips and advice I can. To be asked by the younger professionals is flattering, because it shows they respect what you do.

All the men in this chapter have earned my admiration for being able to do the job at the top level.

MARK BRIGHT

Mark has been a major influence on my career. He was my striking partner when we played together at Crystal Palace. In many ways I was in awe of him because he had played with Gary Lineker at Leicester, so that put pressure on me

to live up to that sort of standard. He taught me so much about professionalism, about a disciplined approach. He has put me on the right road and given me the will to succeed.

From those early days we have remained good, close friends. He is a great professional, a good teacher, and an exceptional forward. He always gets his fair share of goals, no matter which club he plays for. He's very strong in the air and a great all-rounder. In my opinion Mark is one of the best forwards over the last twenty years never to have played for his country.

ANDY COLE

Andy has done amazingly well in his first season at the top, with more than forty magnificent goals. I'm keeping my fingers crossed that he can do as well every season, but it will be a difficult peak to maintain and a very big test. He has been built up into a big star now and people are waiting for him to fall. I hope he doesn't give them the satisfaction. If he is on song next season and can produce maybe twenty-five or thirty goals, he will really establish his high-scoring reputation. But he has to realise that he's not going to produce forty goals every season. Defenders know his game now, and managers and coaches will have planned how to stop him. People will be looking out for him. Perhaps by marking Peter Beardsley tighter, they might cut the supply

Mark Bright has been one of the best striking partners I've ever had. We never won the FA Cup when we were at Palace together but we've both won a few medals in the game since then.

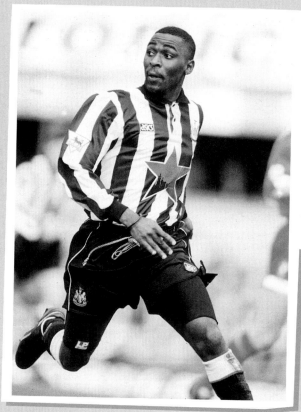

I know somebody who has both Andy Cole and myself in their Fantasy League team. They have clocked up a lot of points on the back of goals scored in real life.

to Andy, but Newcastle have a lot of good all-round players, all of whom can get the ball into the box where this striker does best work.

Of course if he *does* score that many again, hats off! Out of this world. But I think twenty-five goals should be his target, with twenty of those being in the League. Maybe he can produce up to thirty in a good season, and with a good Cup run. That's the target I set myself each season. I wish him well.

DAVID HIRST

David has had very bad luck with injuries at Sheffield Wednesday, just as he was finding his feet in the England team. I personally believe that if it hadn't been for those injuries he'd have left all of us in his wake. If he'd been fit, we'd all be chasing to be his partner for England - David would be the Number One. He has the pace, he holds it up, he's a good header - he can do everything a striker needs to do. And being left-sided he gives a side balance. By all accounts he will be back soon.

David Hirst is a special talent. I just hope he recovers from his long list of injuries. If he can, I suspect he will soon be back in the top bracket of strikers who average a goal every other game.

MARK HUGHES

We never used to get on till last season. For some reason we would always be rowing on the pitch. But Paul Ince always told me he was a nice chap, and when I met him at a Sports Personality Awards Dinner, I had to admit Incey was right.

I admire his positive attitude and his finishing skill. He has played for some of the biggest clubs but Manchester United seems to suit him best. Great enthusiasm is a key quality for strikers. We have to relish the challenge.

Mark is also a flamboyant goalscorer. All his goals have 'Mark Hughes' stamped on them. Great volleys from long distances are his trademark. He's very strong and has a mean streak. He's also a big-occasion player and a match-winner, as he showed, for example, with that last-minute goal against Oldham in the FA Cup semi-final. 'Cometh the hour, cometh the man', as that great saying goes and it's certainly true of football. For example when Mark scored for Manchester United in the European Cup Winners' final and without that late goal against Oldham in the semi-final I think their season would have been over. They'd have been out of the FA Cup, and I reckon they would have lost the League - Blackburn would have won it. But Mark's goal gave Man United the draw, and they easily won the replay 4-1.

Mark Hughes and I have made our peace. I can't remember what we rowed about in the first place, it seems such a long time ago. I'd call him a friend now.

58

Links has not made too
many appearances for
his Japanese side,
Grampus Eight, because
of a toe complaint. Every
England fan will know
just what a contribution
he made with his goals
for his country.

GARY LINEKER

Another big influence. Just to watch him was an education. In many ways I was unfortunate he was around; for one thing I know Graham Taylor didn't think we could play on the same team. With Gary's finishing skill, I was often left on the bench. Naturally I didn't agree with that decision, and if we had played together it would certainly have been interesting. I think the pair of us could have produced a lot of goal-mouth action.

Talking to Gary, I learned a lot about how and when to run into spaces, about trying to outwit defenders, and about being in the right place when the ball flashes across the penalty box. He taught me a few things, did The Boy Lineker.

ALAN SHEARER

The main man. Mature, strong, good attitude - he is a leader. And despite his maturity he joins in all the laughs as well - it's amazing. When he moved to Blackburn for what was then a record fee of £3.6 million, I knew he was a good player all right, but he has improved from there in his two years with his new club. He maintains a certain high standard that he never dips below. He works hard. One of the best finishers around, no

Some player, Alan Shearer. He scores so many goals that Blackburn and England always have a better chance when he's playing.

question. He actually surprised me with the number of goals he's scored, and I'm glad he proved me wrong.

ALAN SMITH

A great player and a genuine nice guy. You never hear him swear or raise his voice. He's only been booked once in his whole career. He has an unselfish attitude, holding the ball up and laying it off for his team-mates. When I first joined Arsenal I settled in straight away: he made so many opportunities for me that I scored a sackful of goals and it went brilliantly for me. Never once did Alan show any jealousy or bitterness. He carried on taking the knocks, holding the ball up, getting kicked. I got the headlines but he got my respect. I have learned a lot from his attitude and application. My own disciplinary record over

the years may have left something to be desired, but I've improved these days, and learned a lot about temperament from Alan Smith.

CHRIS WADDLE

When I was beginning to make my name at Crystal Palace and getting it into a few headlines, I met Chris at a PFA function and he spoke to me for over two hours, just about the game. He has a really great insight into football. He put into words many of the thoughts I had, especially about finishing. He told me that the difference between a striker in the first and second divisions was all about the quality of their finishing. He paid me a big compliment, saying he thought I had what it takes to move up a grade. But he also said it would depend on me. How much did I really want to achieve my ambitions? How much

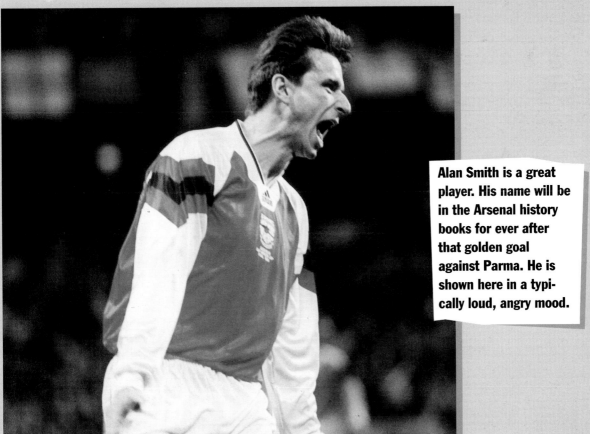

Alan Smith is a great player. His name will be in the Arsenal history books for ever after that golden goal against Parma. He is shown here in a typically loud, angry mood.

work and practice on the training ground was I prepared to put in?

I could watch Chris play all day. He is a joy. I would like to have played in the same teams as him because I'm sure we could have developed a very good understanding and he would have created a lot of chances for me. He is first-class at crossing the ball into the penalty area, and strikers always depend on the quality of the service they get here. Occasionally you can make a goal out of nothing by beating a few players, but mostly your goals are the result of teamwork.

That talk I had with Chris is still vivid in my memory. It really got my mind focused and was to be very influential. That was in the mid-1980s and about five years later, when I was in the England squad, to have him there too was really an amazing plus. I think I owe him a lot.

Not a striker in the accepted fashion but Chris Waddle is a forward with great flair for all that. A very original thinker about the game, I would not be at all surprised if he were a big success as a coach or manager.

CHAPTER TWELVE

FANS

I've always said that football is meant to be entertaining and this is something I believe very strongly. Of course winning is what it's all about and I am a bad loser. When it comes to a choice between being on the winning or the losing side, I'll choose winning every time. But the game can be played in an entertaining way too.

Football is an industry that competes with many other forms of leisure entertainment. We are all trying to capture the imagination of the public, and win a share of their money. So football needs to deliver the goods.

There is so much football on television these days that you can easily imagine the average fan not bothering to go to matches any more. He might just as well sit at home and watch it all on

Arsenal can always rely on tremendous support. At the Cup Winners' Cup Final our fans easily outnumbered those that had travelled from Parma.

We had just won an FA Cup semi-final against Spurs at Wembley and this banner tells the story. Yes, it really was all Wright on the night, even if it was an after-noon kick-off.

It was a strange experience playing in front of the mural. Noise was coming from three sides of the ground only, because the North Bank had been silenced. I was glad when we had fans back at that end of the ground although I think Arsenal rightly got some credit because it was a good idea to cover up all the cranes and diggers.

TV. This is why it is so important to give the public a reason to come along and enjoy the atmosphere, and you do that by providing exciting and entertaining football.

I know the players and followers of many other sports are very envious of the amount of public and press attention given to football. They would be happy to knock us off our perch. I for one don't want to give them the chance.

If I have one little moan about our fans it's when they start to give an Arsenal player a hard time. In fact it doesn't often happen to our club - I know many other clubs that have it far worse than we do. I understand how the fans feel, of course. They pay good money to watch their

clubs, and I suppose this gives them the right to go to town on anyone if they think fit.

But when it comes to criticising Arsenal, or anyone in that famous red shirt, I believe our supporters should give us the benefit of the doubt - at least for ninety minutes. We're doing our best for them. OK, criticise what went wrong after the final whistle, but during the game I don't think moaning does any good.

When we win a big match, the celebrations that follow are shared by us all - players, club and fans. I hope everyone feels on these occasions that we are all in this together. We need one another, after all.

CHAPTER THIRTEEN

Cup Winners' Cup Glory

After our famous 1-0 victory over Parma I was so happy for Alan Smith. What a great servant to Arsenal he has been. And when he scored that winning goal I have to admit that in the dressing room afterwards I was a little bit tearful. After all the help and encouragement he has given me it couldn't have happened to a nicer fellow.

We always thought we could win it but, as the season went on, becoming the only English club left in the European competition provided a great motivation for us. Besides, we had been counted out for all the other honours, so we had put ourselves under pressure to win this one. Our season would have been over had we been knocked out: in fact we wouldn't even have been playing in Europe this season.

The match which best illustrates our awareness of the special demands of Europe came when we beat Standard Liege 7-0 in their own back yard. We were totally on our game that night and confidence went through the roof after this result. (Strange to say, but the Boss didn't play me in this one. Occasionally George works in mysterious ways!)

Oh yes - The Final. For me it wasn't to be, was it?

In the semi-final we played PSG of France, and by the second half I had pulled myself together, but it was too late. The caution I had got in the first half meant I was to miss the Final altogether. Some of the opposition players were even taunting me with this during the game.

In our dressing-room at half-time I had to work really hard not to think about missing the Big Match. I needed to put it out of my mind, and concentrate on helping Arsenal into the Final. That was the priority. I would have to leave my personal problems till later. I was down gutted, to say the least.

It cheered me up a little when people spoke to me afterwards and told me I really played well in that second half. It showed that, 'cometh the hour', I could be there to deliver the goods. I think my approach to that second half, at least, showed I was a good professional footballer for Arsenal. Still, I suppose the ideal professional would not have picked up that second caution anyway, so I can't blow my trumpet too loud.

The Final itself, in Copenhagen against Parma, was a strange and very emotional night for me. Even before the game started, I could feel myself welling up inside. But I was consoled by the fact that I'd made a fair-sized contribution to our progress to that match.

After we had won all the players on the rostrum got a chance to lift the trophy and show it

I think I'm the first Arsenal player to lift a trophy with my regulation club suit on. You can see the club crest on the breast pocket. The bobble hat, I have to admit, is my own.

to the fans. Because I was banned from playing I think UEFA may have been unhappy that I too got my hands on the Cup. But I hope they know I didn't mean any disrespect to them.

My contribution was that I had scored in every round, apart from the Final of course. So I felt I deserved my medal. I would certainly have been very disappointed had I been denied it. David Dein, the Arsenal vice-chairman, said he would make sure I got one, so that was good enough for me.

Paul Dickov, one of our substitutes on the night, was on the pitch during the celebrations and actually wanted to give me his medal there and then. I told him: 'Don't be silly. That's your medal. Whatever happened to me, you were meant to have that.' For him to offer it to me was a great gesture, but I could never have taken it. I told him to keep it and treasure it. I couldn't

help thinking it a little strange, though, that I'd played in so many of the European games and Paul, who'd been on the bench, had landed a medal. Good luck to him, but I'm glad the club made sure I got one too. But then that's what you'd expect from the Arsenal. They look after the players. They do things right.

As you may remember, John Jensen was injured and also missed the game, but he was really enjoying the build-up because he is Danish and loved being part of such a big match in his home country, even if he could hardly walk properly. Before the match I was in the players' tunnel but he came and turfed me out to wave to our travelling supporters. I felt better after that. I did my best to stir up even more shouting and cheering for the team, as well. They lifted the Arsenal. I know they lifted me.

Alan Smith, who played almost the perfect game as a lone striker against Parma, takes advantage of a defensive lapse to score from twenty yards.

Arsenal players make a human wigwam when I am first to score in the semi-final in Paris after a brilliant free kick by Paul Davis. Referees seem to be trying to stop these celebrations. I can't see why: everybody enjoys them - apart from your opponents' fans, that is.

There is no mistaking the jubilation on Alan's face. He is about to be mobbed by his team-mates but looks to be running away from them.

CHAPTER FOURTEEN

OUR FUTURE KING

I am a big fan of Prince Charles. Everything about him appeals to me: the way he carries himself is just impeccable. How he dealt with someone taking a pot-shot at him in Australia is one recent example that illustrates just what a man he is.

Here was an upper-crust Englishman at his best. In those few seconds when a lunatic rushed towards him he remained totally unflustered. Instead of being threatened by the gun, Charles remained so calm you would have thought he was being offered a chilled beer. He just carried on twiddling his cuff-links. Amazing.

I love the ring Prince Charles wears on his little finger. George Graham also wears a ring on that finger: perhaps he is emulating Royalty now.

I also think he has great dress sense. Those

I'm only a beginner when it comes to living in a goldfish bowl as Prince Charles does. Most places I go people might recognise me but I'm not always surrounded by media hounds. I've got plenty of freedom to go pretty much wherever I want.

English suits, hand-made and the best quality, look just brilliant in my eyes.

I read a biography of him recently and his early schooldays seemed quite horrible. Few of the boys there would talk to him and if any did they were teased by the others for grovelling. He must have been really lonely. Considering that he was growing up to be the most important man in the country it must have been very hard for him.

I was really gutted that his marriage did not work out. Hopefully in the future things will work out for him.

But for me he is the ultimate, a great role model, a hero even, and I don't care who knows I think like this.

I can't think that our lives have been much alike but I do know a little about living in a goldfish bowl with everyone looking at you. But for him it must be a million times worse and, of course, it started as soon as he was born. I've really only got attention since I moved to Arsenal.

I can understand that need to get away sometimes. When I retire it's on my mind to drive around Europe on a Harley-Davidson. A lot of my friends did this when they were younger, and I feel as if I missed out. Still, if I do it now I know that I could stay in a good hotel and wouldn't have to sleep in a tent unless I wanted to. It's very much in the future but it's an experience I want to have.

At Wembley before FA Cup Finals you are usually introduced to Royalty, often the Duke and Duchess of Kent, and I always look at the shoes the Duke is wearing. They are polished until they shine like a mirror but they could be a hundred years old. Because the shoes are such good quality the fact that they are old only makes the shoes look better. Strange I know, but true.

A madman rushes the platform in Australia where Prince Charles is speaking. There is chaos all around but, like all the best strikers, he remains cool under pressure.

CHAPTER FIFTEEN

THE ENTERTAINERS

Football is part of the entertainment business and I believe the majority of English football clubs put a priority on providing this for their fans. Everybody knows that every club is looking to win as many matches as possible, but there are a few players and clubs that stand out for me when it comes to entertaining football supporters - their own and other clubs'.

PETER BEARDSLEY

This is a player I really, really admire. His attitude is first-rate and he is another role-model for me. I don't think you can instil enthusiasm in players. They either have it or they don't. Peter Beardsley has it - no doubt about that.

We're alike in that we both love training, and playing football. After a few weeks off in the summer, I want to get stuck in again, and Peter is just the same.

He is another unselfish player because he is happy to make goals for others. So many of Andy Cole's goals were laid on the plate by Peter. His close control when dribbling around defenders is such a great asset. Defenders are very cautious about giving away fouls so close to goal, and with that huge support at Newcastle you can sense all those Geordies willing him to do well. The fact that he makes those goals for others doesn't detract from his own goal-scoring record. It stands up over many years, and that is a true test of quality.

BLACKBURN ROVERS

Are they thinking of changing their name to 'The Club that Jack Built'? Every time a big-name player becomes available, they seem to buy him, or at least express an interest in buying him. With Kenny Dalglish spending Jack Walker's money they are strong in every department, from the goalkeeper Tim Flowers to Alan Shearer leading the line.

They are like Arsenal in that they hate giving goals away and, also like us, they place a high priority on good defending - not that we overemphasize this aspect of our game, but it has to be done, let's face it.

RYAN GIGGS

I have every confidence that Ryan will fulfil all expectations of him. He has a great attitude to the game. His love of football shows every time he steps on the field. It is stirring to watch him beating opposition players in a flowing move-

Peter Beardsley would like to play football right the way through the year, with perhaps just a couple of weeks close season. He has always been a top-class player and totally deserved his recall into the England set-up under Terry Venables.

Blackburn Rovers enters the transfer market so often that all these players may have been replaced by the time this book comes out. But I'd be shocked if anyone could take Alan Shearer's place.

ment. Because he plays on the wing for Manchester United and happens to be good-looking into the bargain, many people make comparisons with George Best. I pray that what happened to Best won't happen to Ryan, though I don't think he will allow himself to go the same way as his great predecessor. Best, let's face it, wasted a God-given talent. Of course, Alex Ferguson will keep an eye on Ryan, but in any case Paul Ince will be watching and just wouldn't let that happen.

MATT LE TISSIER

I have never seen a player who scores goals with such apparent ease as Matt: he makes it look so easy that it's practically frightening! It's not arrogance but it almost seems that way, because although it is in the rules of the game that a goal is scored when the ball goes between the posts, from Matt's reaction you'd think he was hardly bothered half the time. Of course he really does care. It's just Matt's style to look 'laid-back'. He is trying, just as hard as the player whose facial expression is one of torture and agony. But he looks cool and calm, even when he's scoring out-of-this-world goals. He is a top entertainer, and Southampton fans are lucky to have a player like him on their doorstep.

MANCHESTER UNITED

The yardstick by which all other clubs are judged - at the moment, anyway - must be Manchester United. They show that you can get results and provide entertainment at the same time. I can quite imagine that many players in other clubs would want to play for them. Man United looks as if it can do anything it likes with the opposition. They toy with them sometimes.

Young Ryan is a wing-wizard who is really going places, not only down the wing at a rate of knots but also stepping out with good-looking girls.

Matt is really trying here, you can see it on his face, and these two Chelsea defenders are history. Don't be fooled by his laid-back approach: he wants to win.

I like Eric Cantona very much. At the end of last season he showed that, despite trouble with the refs and with sendings-off and suspensions, he could handle the pressure, come back and still be central to everything in the team's title run-in. Great player. Quality player. He shows tremendous understanding towards those receiving a pass from him. The ball is placed right in their path so that they don't have to struggle to control it. He just delivers it to their feet.

The club's next big test will be to turn their success in domestic football into European glory. I don't see any reason they shouldn't. I know we hear a lot about Italian football, but if United have won the title here two years running - I don't care what anyone says - that makes them an outstanding side.

NEWCASTLE UNITED

Kevin Keegan has rescued this club. It has always enjoyed huge support but now those supporters have a team to cheer for. I like their approach to the game - they are very attacking, and all of their players like to get forward. Quite the right strategy when you consider Cole and Beardsley lead their forward line.

Some of their passing movements, especially around the opponents' penalty areas, are so quick and inventive I see no reason why they can't at last establish themselves as a major force and always be up there chasing honours.

NORWICH CITY

Some people may think this a strange choice under the 'Entertainers' heading, but I can't stand it when fans look at the fixture list and say, 'Norwich - oh, that'll be an easy three points!'.

These people must be mad - they certainly don't know anything about football. On their day, Norwich can beat anyone. They can look like Brazil! And when the team is on song, you hardly get a touch. I have a lot of respect for their approach. They have played brilliantly. Maybe they aren't one of the really big clubs, because of their location and the fact that they can't attract large crowds. But they are a credit to English football. Ask Bayern Munich if you are in any doubt!

Here we go again, trotting back to the half-way line after another Newcastle goal. They were the top scorers in the Premiership last season, with eighty-two goals. 'Haway the Lads!'

If you get a chance to see Norwich play, take it. They may never win the European Cup but I think you are almost guaranteed an entertaining match. Here their Nigerian international Efan Ekoku slips away from a Wimbledon defender.

CHAPTER SIXTEEN

My Best Friend

It is often said that you can have acquaintances in football but not friends. I disagree. Paul Ince and I first played against each other for West Ham and Crystal Palace respectively and when Palace played United in the FA Cup Final we came to respect each other's play. But it wasn't until we were in the same England squad that we hit it off.

Most club players will share hotel rooms so that you have someone to talk to when you are miles from home, and avoid boredom setting in. But Graham Taylor used to let us choose. A lot of the England players went for single rooms, but Paul and I have so much in common that it seems natural for us to share. We are both single-minded; both have a very strong will to win. In Paul's case a lot of this motivation comes from the time when he had what might have been a career-threatening injury - when he moved from West Ham to Manchester United in 1990. He realises how lucky he was. Perhaps this has helped him maintain his drive.

Look at Paul now - and you can't think of a Manchester United or an England side without him in it. It's impossible.

It was a slightly different route into professional football for me, but I know my own luck,

If we were giving marks for artistic impression this effort would score pretty high, even if the shot itself went miles wide.

too. I climbed into the game from a building site. When I had my first trial, at Brighton, I was nineteen. I lost my building job because I'd taken two months off work to prepare for that trial. So when two years later Palace invited me to attend a trial for them, I nearly didn't go. It all worked out in the end, but it was very risky. I didn't suddenly wake up one morning and find myself playing for Arsenal. These experiences make Paul and me grab the chances that come our way. We make the most of them.

In the summer we both had tattoos of a Harley-Davidson done on our thighs. We say we're not blood brothers, we're Tattoo Brothers! You won't be able to see the workmanship as the designs don't come below our football shorts.

George Graham doesn't share the Tattoo Brothers' enthusiasm for motor bikes. He won't let me have a real Harley-Davidson at the moment, so this is the closest I can get. When George first told me his decision I didn't agree with it, but now I've had a chance to think it over, I have to admit he's right - as usual. Supposing I had an accident - you can imagine the trouble I'd be in, and the consequences for the club. When I retire from football, though, there will be a life-size Harley-Davidson waiting for me - my present to myself. All shining and silver power.

Incey and I are always on the phone to each other. The first thing Paul will do is complain about something. Once he's got that off his chest, though, he's all right. Many fans know only what they see of us on television and, yes, Paul does look as if he's moaning most of the time. But that's not the real Incey.

I know some football fans probably think we're both flash and horrible, but I don't think you get the right impression from television images. If Manchester United are in a live TV game, I might see Paul flare up over a small incident, and when we talk about it on the phone soon afterwards I do tell him that it doesn't improve his popularity. We try to keep each other in line. We are good for each other in that respect: we offer constructive criticism of each other's behaviour.

Some people make friends for life at school: well, though Paul and I didn't meet that far back, I think we'll be lifelong friends.

Nothing lightens up a training session like a spot of the tango. To be quite honest, I have no idea what was going on here. I'm wondering if this picture wasn't made up in a lab somewhere.

This, I think, is how most fans would picture Paul. He is going into a tackle and he plans to win it. In England we would say this type of tackle is hard but fair, although in Europe a foul would almost certainly be given against you.

CHAPTER SEVENTEEN

THE FAMILY

Towards the end of last season I was playing for England in our match against Norway. Soon after the game I got the news that I was waiting to hear: my wife Deborah had given birth to a son - our first, Stacey.

All the lads in the Wembley dressing-room offered their congratulations and I really did feel that there was no happier man in the world. If that sounds soppy, well OK, so what? That's exactly how I felt.

Debs and I grew up on the same south London estate, so we have roots in common. Our relationship owes nothing to my fame, or money, or any of the attention that my name sometimes attracts. We both know where we're coming from. We lost touch for a while, but met up by accident at a bus stop about five years ago. And that was that, really.

From a previous relationship I have Bradley and Brett and an adopted boy, Shaun. Bradley is showing some promising signs on the football pitch, and I hear a few clubs are taking a look at him already.

Nothing would please me more than if any of my boys wanted a career in football, but they will not be allowed to think that because they are the sons of a footballer they have an automatic ticket into the game. In fact it would probably be more difficult for them than for other boys, because sportsmen's sons often have a hard time being accepted in their own right. I can just imagine how it would be if Bradley was training with Arsenal. Some clubs have a better record than others for bringing kids on, and this would have to be taken into consideration. Impossible to fault Arsenal on that one!

My wife Debs has her own distinctive style, and has made a brilliant job of having our home redecorated. She's very independent and it's nice when she tells me I haven't changed since we first met. That shows I'm not bigheaded, doesn't it?

Mr & Mrs Ian Wright

CHAPTER EIGHTEEN

THE BOSS

When George Graham and Arsenal wanted to sign me from Crystal Palace I didn't need to think twice. I thought then that they were the biggest club in London and I still do. David Rocastle was at the club at that time and he has remained a good friend. He comes from the same area as me and I knew I would be made welcome straight away. Although he is now at Manchester City we are often in touch and he is god-father to my youngest boy.

I've seen that George has said I make him both laugh and cry and I have tried to work out in my own mind what this means - or what I hope it means.

In the dressing-room or on the coach with all the players there are so many jokes going round that it creates a really good atmosphere and I think George can appreciate that I do my bit to keep spirits up, and anyway I think he likes my sense of humour.

But how do I make him cry? Well, perhaps it's when he reckons I could do just that little bit better on the pitch.

He has a special way of getting the best out of me. Yes, he shouts at me! At half-time he can give me a really good talking to, but we both know that this is the best way of geeing me up. So many times I've gone out in the second half and scored a goal or two.

At first I have to say that I was just ignorant of what he was trying to do. But this approach has worked so many times that now I have to agree he knows what he's doing. His management of me is first class.

The other Arsenal players do it too. They give me stick during the game, especially Paul Merson, but it helps me, so for me that's just fine.

All players are different and respond to differing approaches, but George is just right for me. A day or so after the match he will explain why he said what he said and everything is suddenly much clearer.

The Boss and I are always commenting on each other's clothes. He certainly has a lot of ties and, although I would like to think I'm the smartest dresser at Arsenal, in all fairness I have to say that the Boss does dress very well.

I can't quite say the same for Ray Parlour. Whatever he's wearing he doesn't look good. To be fair to Ray I think he's just not bothered about things like this.

When it comes to football I think George and I are alike. We are both perfectionists and like testing ourselves against the best and that means playing against the top teams of Europe and beating them. We are never completely satisfied unless we taste victory in Europe, so that is why Arsenal's Cup Winners' Cup victory was so important.

I missed out on selection for the 1990 World

This is George Graham, Arsenal manager, very well dressed and with a nice tie, holding the old League Championship trophy. I think by now he must be judged the most successful manager in the club's history.

Cup squad and if I am not involved in France in 1998 it will leave a big gap in my career, because I want to test myself on the big stages. I believe there's no point in competing without that attitude.

So, until that time, Arsenal's matches in European competition will provide the stiff challenges that George and I both need.

Two sides of the Boss. One of the questions I'm always being asked is what George Graham is like. These two pictures give the answer. Yes, he has a sense of humour but without a shadow of a doubt he can be serious when he needs to be. (I remain to be convinced by the short white socks.)

If I make George laugh and cry maybe this is the picture that did it. I can just imagine his reaction if I wanted to play in this wig. I don't think I would get within ten miles of Highbury. He would even man the road-block himself!

'OK Boss, I get the message: a hat-trick before half-time and then you want me to really concentrate on my game in the second half.'

CHAPTER NINETEEN

NEIGHBOURS

The meeting of the capital's two top clubs has been called by some 'The Battle of London'. I'm not madly keen on using expressions like that to describe a football match. Make no mistake, though - after one of these derby matches you know you have been in a game.

The grounds of Arsenal and Tottenham are only three miles apart, so you can easily see how this intense rivalry has grown up over more than a century. These are big matches that everybody, players and fans alike, relishes and looks forward to.

You will probably be surprised to learn that I never get any trouble from Spurs fans. I am not stupid enough to think they are going to like me - that would be expecting too much! - but once we get into conversation we get along just fine. I can't say as much of other London clubs. I wish I could, but I can't.

Sometimes Spurs fans pay me the biggest compliment of all when they tell me how they wish I played for them. There is no way I could ever imagine that situation arising, but for the fans to make such a comment gives me a lot of pleasure and satisfaction.

I usually try to remind them that I have a very good record of scoring last-minute goals against Tottenham! We have a laugh over this. Well, I laugh, anyway.

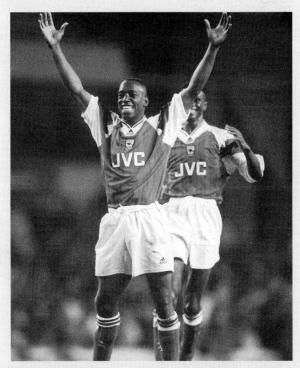

Arms aloft, grin on my face, that usually means I've scored a goal. Extra-large grin on my face and I've scored against Spurs. It's a special feeling and on the pitch you can sense our supporters willing us on.

Just because he's got a Spurs shirt on doesn't mean I can't recognise a good player when I see one. Darren Anderton was on top form last season and, with Terry Venables seeming to like his style of wing play, he has a very bright future. And he's a nice lad as well.

Trying to burst past defenders using pace over the first few yards gives goalscorers a vital edge. It is an essential quality in the modern game.

Let's say that at the very least Arsenal-Spurs matches are keenly contested. Because there are so many London clubs in the top flight and with the games being so competitive, we often drop points against each other. This makes it harder to mount a serious challenge for the title, though in the next few seasons I see us really going for it.

CHAPTER TWENTY

THE WRIGHT REPORT
WORLD CUP '94

In Bologna, Italy, late in 1993, England defeated San Marino 7-1 in a World Cup qualifying match. I had scored four goals but was in no mood to celebrate.

Just after the final whistle news came through that the Dutch had won in Poland and so our last slim chance of making it to the US had now gone. England's World Cup campaign had ended almost before it had begun. Norway and Holland had qualified from our group, leaving us in World Cup limbo. Graham Taylor's resignation followed soon afterwards.

In the dressing-room everybody felt a deep sense of disappointment. Professionally and personally it was a low point. The World Cup is the biggest stage of all and we had all desperately wanted an opportunity to show what we could do. But in the end we could only watch from the side-lines.

If I felt disappointed then, my feelings having watched the tournament and all the excitement it has created are of almost total misery. My family and the prospect of future honours with

Arsenal have kept me going and my spirits up, although I don't think my frustration at not playing in the World Cup of 1994 will ever really leave me.

When it was first announced that America were going to be hosting the World Cup my immediate reaction was that it was a terrible idea. I thought they would let razzmatazz take over and that the actual football would be buried. I also dreaded the idea of the world's best players playing matches in front of small crowds.

How wrong I was! How little I knew! It was a fantastic competition - great crowds, great matches. But the undoubted success of the tournament just makes it all the sadder for those not involved. Even the matches involving what you could only call the smaller countries attracted brilliant crowds. Oh, to have been there!

When I watch matches, naturally I always look at what the strikers are doing, but I also take a special interest in the midfield players. I try to imagine how, if we were in the same team, we would play together and, most importantly, how many chances would be made for me.